How to start and Grow Your Business

For

Profit

I0486210

ABOUT THE AUTHOR

Evuetapha Oghenekparobo Godwin is an Inspirational and Multi-gifted speaker and writer, an Entrepreneur and a business Consultant. He addresses issues concerning entrepreneurship, social, personal and thinking development. He is the founder of Elite Business Minds, KP concepts and a supporter of Job Creation Initiatives and many other Business Ventures.
He inspires millions of people far and near and in the world at large through his great books and networks. His unique and exceptional abilities to connect to the world originate from his passion to tackle challenges facing the society and the world at large.

This book will change your status. Happy reading

He is open to suggestions and feedbacks. For further Enquiries send an email to

        +234(0)903-826-0849

Content

INTRODUCTION

Starting a business is not as hard as most people thinks. If you have the means to kickoff; capital, technical knowhow and other necessary skills required to keep and sustain that business and thrive in it, it is only a matter of dedication and persistency.

However, starting a business has been a phobia for many people due to the following fears: dealing with people, financial security, fear of failure, fear of uncertainties. Those who are able to start a business find themselves with the next big challenge; that is, how can they grow the business and make profit?

These challenges are usually the primary challenge every future successful business owner/entrepreneur tackles and solve before starting a successful business. The challenges are;

1. How do I start the business? (Combining every factor necessary to put the business in the market place).

2. How do I grow the business for profit? (This is about customers' attraction, marketing, sales, profit and business expansion/growth).

Entrepreneur's note
Starting a business has been a phobia for many people due to the following fears; dealing with people, financial security, fear of failure, fear of uncertainties.

With this two major challenge to tackle, this 'success in business classics' will be structured to tackle both challenges in the order in which they are listed above in subsequent sections.

Reports on business success rate by business experts, business journals and financial institutions show that 80% of start-ups close before the end of their 3rd year in business. As much as this report holds true, however, the category of business and the cause of failure is not stated to give an actual cause of failure.

It is important to know that most of these businesses close for one or more of the following factors:

1. Lack of funds.
2. Lack of skilled personnel/manpower.

3. Lack of adequate knowledge about the business.

4. Lack of good customer service.

5. Being in a business they have no business or personal skill that ensures their success.

Each of these factors is crucial to the level of success a business can attain. Inadequacy of any of these factors may result to inability to start the business (for Starters) or failure of the business or bankruptcy of an already existing business.

An entrepreneur must know how these factors work and how to provide each of these factors in a situation where they are unavailable.

You have to note that factors (1) & (2) i.e. Capital and skilled personnel/manpower can be gotten or borrowed at one point or another during the course of starting/running a business.

Also factors (4) & (5) i.e. lack of good customer service and being in the wrong business can be taken care of if factor (3) (i.e. Adequate knowledge about the business) is well understood and mastered by the pioneer of the business.

Research shows that for every 100 people that go into business, more than 70% of them do not know how to get their Initial Capital back, Rate of Returns and how to put the business on track when it is going in circles (not making meaningful progress).

If you belong to such a group, it shows that you are using the Trial and Error Approach to business or what we call the "shoot first and ask questions later". The probability of the trial and error approach to produce the desired outcome is 0.01%. This is a very slim probability and no entrepreneur who wants to succeed should gamble his/her Time, Money and other resources on this kind of outcome.

Everyone who wants to be successful in business and in life needs to have an adequate knowledge of these three (3) parameters:

1. Where they are now (Present Situations)

2. Where they are going to (Future of the business), and

3. How they can be able to get there (Process of getting there).

Simply put, you have to know your present situation and environment, your destination/future and what it should look like and finally, the process involve in getting to the desired destination.

Factor (3), that is, having adequate knowledge about the perceived business supersedes every other factor. As you may already know, it's not the acquisition of knowledge that produces the desired results, but the application of the relevant knowledge acquired. We will discuss adequate knowledge in the next chapter.

1 ADEQUATE KNOWLEDGE ABOUT THE BUSINESS

This involves knowing what to render your present/future customers based on their present and future needs and wants.

As an entrepreneur, you must acknowledge that in today's Competitive Market, the customers are king and are the major reason why you are in business. Every successful or potential successful entrepreneur always asks themselves; how can I satisfy my customers and do it better than any competitors? Without such question at the back of your mind you will be going into business to satisfy yourself alone and not your customers.

Please Note: *satisfying yourself may generate one sale or no sale, but satisfying your customers may generate millions of sales.*

When using the customers' satisfaction principle as the basis of building your business, you need to answer the following questions:

1. Who are my Potential Customers?

2. What are my Customers' Wants and Needs?

3. How will I be able to meet their Wants and Needs?

4. Does my Potential Customers already have a business they patronize (Your Competitors)?

5. How will I be able to provide better services than my Competitors?

An effective solution to the questions mentioned above, will ensure you succeed in starting your business (if you are starting), and also, grow your business for profit such that the business will continually operate for decades to come. In today's competitive world of business, it's all about the clients/customers and how you can satisfy/meet their demands.

1.1 Technical Know-how

Successfully starting and running of a business requires knowing the process the business has to take from the point of inception where you invest your Time, Money and Effort to the point where you make sales, generate revenue or have returns on investments.

Age wrinkle the body. Quitting wrinkles the Soul - Douglas MacArthur

This is what we call the '*System* of the Business' or
"*business System*".

Simply put, a business system is a process/path a
business takes from the initial inputs to outputs or to
the point where a sale is made or profit attained.
It is important to note that one reason why a *Profit
Oriented* business is setup is to make profit or at least
an amount that will keep you and your business
from bankruptcy, so be *Profit Oriented*, but *don't cheat*
your customers so that they don't lose trust in you,
*also give them the best possible price in both parties best
interest.*

For a restaurant owner that sells soft drinks, his
system may be the following:

1. Purchasing of the soft drinks from distributors,

2. Transporting it down to his business outlet,

3. Storing it in a cold room or refrigerator and finally,

4. Selling it to customers for *cash*.

When he gets to the end of the process, he repeats the cycle over and over again. This is his *system* of making money.

So when you have gotten a proper understanding of the system your business requires, you need to replicate it and fine-tune it to be more profitable to you and more satisfying to your customers.

*Please Note **that** different systems may be required for:*

different business or same kind of business in different

location or same kind of business with different

Motives/Aim.

2 SKILLS REQUIRED FOR SUCCESS IN BUSINESS

Skills are the technical input an individual (entrepreneur) has to put into a business or business system to make it productive and successful. Different skills set are required for different kind of business or different business systems. The skill set needed to effectively operate a Law Firm will be different from the ones needed to operate a Medical Centre.

However, we are going to briefly discuss the general skills an entrepreneur, Venture Capitalist or Business Owner should posses in order to succeed in today's competitive world of business.

2.1 Business Success Skills

They are listed below in no particular order of importance:

- ➢ Negation Skill

- ➢ Art of Selling

- ➢ Persuasion Skill

- ➢ Leadership Skill

- ➢ Managerial Skill

- ➢ Good Communication

- ➢ Problem Solving Skill

- ➢ Social Skills

- ➢ Strategic Thinking/Planning

Let's discuss each of these skills briefly:

❖ Negotiation Skill: This is a vital skill a good
leader, Entrepreneur, Venture Capitalist and
business owner should posses and master in
order to succeed in business. Negotiation
involves seeking for/getting concessions and
values that are important to you from the
other party and giving out values or
concession to the other party to have a win-
win situation.

Note that there are also a win-lose, lose-win,
lose-lose situations which is not good for you
if you want to continually remain in business.
In business and life situations, people are on a
daily basis using negotiation tactics against
you whether you are aware of it or not. Your
best protection against this is to be a good

negotiator as well, so as not to fall prey to other skilled negotiators.

In the past, you may have find yourself in a situation where you are trying to purchase something you admire or doing a deal with someone and as soon as you ask a concession; be it a fair price, material things etc, the other party reply may go like this, "that's not a bad thing to ask, however my boss won't allow it" or "Gosh, my boss will fire me if I do that (looking surprise)" or "Let me speak to my Wife or Husband about it".

This is called the *Final Decision-Maker Technique,* it is used to make you bend over and agree to their Terms. I guess you may not have heard of this technique, now you know, and there are other techniques as far as negotiation is concern, Like the *"Good Guy*

Bad Guy Technique" etc.

✦ Art of Selling: Buying and selling is part of

our everyday activities. As a profit oriented

organization, selling is not to be left in the

hands of inexperience sales personnel, the use

of Trial and Error Approach will cost you

more than you can bear. If you are going to

sell whatever products or services your

company offers, then you have to put in time

and energy to do it well and get it right so as

to get the right results.

Most business outlet with good products and services to offer its customers fail and go bankrupt because of *Ineffective Sales Strategy and Sales Personnel.*

It is important to note that the sales department is the backbone of every company, because without it, there will be no sale and such business will fold up in no distant time.

As an Entrepreneur, *you need to know, master and harness the art of Selling to your advantage and be efficient at doing it all the time, every time.* Your business life depends on it, your employees' life depends on it and your life and that of those depending on you for survival depends on it as well.

Take courses on this and be good at it.

❖ Persuasion Skill: persuasion is making someone else see things from your perspective. The world is full of people from diverse backgrounds, and at such, so are their mindsets, beliefs and perceptions about whatever they see; including what you and your business are offering. Your ability to persuade them so that both of you can be on a common footing, the better it will be for you to not only make a sale, but have them as customers for life.

Some persons are usually on a defensive mindset when they approach a business outlet, your job is to make them less defensive and put both of you on "common grounds" to break their defensive mindset. A mastery and effective utilization of this skill will sets your business in a better position financially than other businesses/entrepreneur that lacks this skill.

❖ Leadership Capabilities: a Leader is someone who guides and develops the activities of others and seeks to provide continual training and direction.

Leadership is a discipline of deliberately exerting special influence within a group to move it towards goals of beneficial permanence that fulfil the group's real needs.

Without good leaders in an organization, things don't get done as it ought to. An organization with no leader is like a gathering of sheep with no shepherd to guide them. You know there will be chaos among the flocks.

As an Entrepreneur, you need to develop good leadership skills and use such skill to run your business effectively by leading well. Note that the best form of leadership is leadership by example. This is because it has been proven scientifically that people mirror your actions and behaviours i.e. people will most likely do what they see you do and not what they have been told to do, this mirror effect takes place unconsciously to them. So be a good leader, lead yourself well and your followers as well.

❖ Managerial Abilities: this is the ability to combine all factors of production effectively to produce the desired result.

While using your managerial abilities, you are responsible for looking after and getting the best out of a team which may sometimes behave like children and you have to put them to order.

You are responsible for a group of people from diverse background that you may not like, might have nothing in common with and you have to coax out of them a decent day's work.

Without good management in place, the system responsible for the smooth running of the business collapses and it is the duty of the

business owner to fix this or restore this

system, even if he/she is not the acting

manager. This is one reason why managerial

abilities are important to an entrepreneur.

❖ Good Communication: this is very vital to the

success of any organization. Humans are

social beings that thrive on good and effective

communication. Without good

communication, there will be chaos in an

organization.

Communication can be:

1. Internal Communication

2. External Communication

As an Entrepreneur, you need this skill to communicate with your employees within your organization and to your clients and customers outside your organization.

You need be good in the following aspects of communication:

1. General Conversation

2. Courtesy

3. Diplomacy.

★ ★ ★ ★ ★ ★ ★ ★ ★ ★

Entrepreneurs' note

Without good communication, there will be chaos in an organization.

★ ★ ★ ★ ★ ★ ★ ★ ★ ★

❖ Problem Solving Abilities: As long as one is alive, problems are bound to occur from various angles, same goes for running a business. Your ability to deal with these problems and provide adequate solutions as fast as possible will determine the efficiency of your organization and ultimately, its success. As an Entrepreneur, it is important to note that every problem that arises is a challenge begging to be resolved, and with every challenge, comes hidden opportunities waiting to be exploited.

Develop this skill and use it to your advantage.

* * * * * * * * * *

Entrepreneurs' note

It is important to note that every problem that arises is a challenge begging to be resolved, and with every challenge, comes hidden opportunities waiting to be exploited.

* * * * * * * * * *

❖ Social Skills: This involves connecting with people within and outside your organization. A man with better social skill will be '*liked*' by more people and will *attract* people, customers, deals etc, to himself and his organization.

Note that business is a *likeness* game. If people like you and feel comfortable with you, they will do business with you over and over

★ ★ ★ ★ ★ ★ ★ ★ ★ ★
Entrepreneurs' note
A man with better social skill will be liked by more people and will attract people, customers, deals etc, to himself and his organization.
★ ★ ★ ★ ★ ★ ★ ★ ★ ★

again and most of all, they will refer your business to their friends and colleague. Now that's an advert you didn't have to pay for,

just by using this skill properly.

❖ Strategic Thinking and Planning: this involve

thoroughly thinking situations through;

considering every possible outcome to get the

best fit solution before making a decision or

taking action.

Strategic planning involve considering every

minute detail in your planning process and

knowing how each parameter affect the

desired outcome.

Strategic Thinking and Planning are good

because it makes your business more efficient

in getting the desired outcome and also it

helps you know which parameter to alter to

put your business on track and make more

profit in lesser time.

An entrepreneur with strategic thinking

ability will be more aware of hidden

opportunities and will position his business

on a better footing to be more profitable.

❖ Diplomacy: this is under communication, but

it is so important that we have to treat it

specially.

Diplomacy is <u>not</u> the art of lie telling. It is the

art of presenting a potentially bad situation or

scenario that can affect you and your business

negatively in a manner that such situation

doesn't sound as bad as it really is to

outsiders or your investors.

Diplomacy is the art of letting someone have

your way. In diplomacy, you learn "*double-

talk*" or as a writer Emily Dickenson once

wrote, "Tell the truth but tell it slant".

It is important to note that this skill should

not be used too often unless when necessary,

otherwise you won't be taken seriously.

A notable man who displays an amazing

ability to adapt under conditions of great

stress and pressure is Winston Churchill. He mastered the language of a leader and peppered his diplomacy with humour. When he was facing the tyranny of Adolph Hitler, Churchill said, *"An appeaser is one who feeds a crocodile, hoping it eats him last."*
This helped him rally more support from his people.

You need to learn and master this skill as an entrepreneur; you never can tell when you may need it to save the day or know when

★ ★ ★ ★ ★ ★ ★ ★ ★ ★
Entrepreneurs' note
Diplomacy is not the art of lie telling
★ ★ ★ ★ ★ ★ ★ ★ ★ ★

someone is using it on you and how to counter theirs.

2.2 Personal Success Skills

As important as possessing business skills are to

handling and succeeding in business, so also are

Personal Success Skills; which are vital to make you

succeed in business and in life. Know that the

business will not operate itself without the

entrepreneur directing its activities, using his

personal success skills to do so.

The following are Personal Success Skills an

Entrepreneur should possess and master in order to

be efficient and Successful in his dealings:

1.   Good Character

2.   Dedication

3.   Persistency

4.   Creativity/innovative abilities

★ ★ ★ ★ ★ ★ ★ ★ ★ ★

Entrepreneurs' note

A business will not operate itself; an entrepreneur is
required to direct its activities, using his personal success

skills to do so.

★ ★ ★ ★ ★ ★ ★ ★ ★ ★

5.   Affability

6.   Open Minded

7.   Cheerful Disposition

8.   Good conversation Ability

9.   Courage

10.   Courtesy

11.   Dignity

12.   Decisive

13.   Emotional Control

14.   Enthusiasm

15.   Fondness for People

16.   Honesty

17.   Honour

18.   Patience

19.   Principle

20.   Observation Abilities

21.   Punctuality

22.   Personal Appearance

23.   Social Ability

24.   Sincerity

25.   Having A pleasing Voice

26.   Diligent/ Hard working

27.   Love

28.   Personal Aspirations/Dream Big

29.   Positive Attitude

30.   Thinking Ability

31.   Visionary ability

32.   Loyalty.

Action Exercise

1. Write/Identify present condition, situation in

your business or Surroundings. List the

challenges facing your business (or potential

business venture).

2. Your business Future: Identify where you

   want your business to be in the next; one

   year, Five years or Ten years from now (Your

   Business Dream/Vision).

3. Write out Goals/path or processes to achieve

   the stated Vision. Provide solutions to

   existing and future challenges facing your

   business Venture.

4. Identify which business skills or and personal

   skills are essential to the success of your

proposed business venture and adopt and

utilize such skills.

5. Take action on these and be consistent until

you produce the desired result.

SECTION A:

STARTING

A

BUSINESS

3 STARTING A BUSINESS

It's not what you do, it's what you get done – Dr Anthony Fei

To be in business, you need to know what a business is, and the steps you need to take to make your business successful. You need to know where you are, where you want to be and the process/path to get there, you need to have a Vision and goals to accomplish that vision. When preparing to start a business, there are lots of questions you need to answer before commencing on this beautiful adventure.

These questions will serve as a guide to you during and after you have started the business. Business has been good to those who know what their aims are and are executing it effectively.

- The First Question to Answer...

    The first question one needs to ask his/her self about is: WHAT IS BUSINESS???

    I know most of you will say you already know what business is and what it's all about but you might be wrong in over assuming

    ★ ★ ★ ★ ★ ★ ★ ★ ★ ★
    Entrepreneurs' note
    ★ ★ ★ ★ ★ ★ ★ ★ ★ ★

    that you know it, just by hearing the word

business. Come to think of it, we have all heard the word business from when we were little until now and have been told different meaning about it, but critically thinking of it, is there more to business than what we have been told in the past? You bet there is. Let's get the definition from the Oxford Advanced Learners Dictionary, it defined business as: the activity of making, buying, selling or supplying goods and services for money. While this is true, in reality, business is much more than just this.

For the purpose of this, we will define business as any undertaking, discussion or bargain that creates *Mutual Benefits To Both Parties Right Now Or In The Near Future.*

Definitely, money has to be involved. But don't forget *mutual benefits*. It starts and ends with it. Without mutual benefits, you are not guaranteed of future patronage.

In essence, when doing business always asks yourself this question in your mind; "what is in for me and what is in it for them?"
If both conditions are met appropriately, i.e. you have something to gain and the other party have something to gain as well then you are in business.

- Second Question: What Does A Business Consist Of?

These are the parameters and things that are to be put in place for business to take place successfully and effectively. These include:

- Land

- Capital

- Human resources etc...

 Of these, the greatest of all is human resources. That includes you and every human being working for you.

They are the ones that will make your business grow, they are the ones who will attend to your customer and make them happy with your products and services. You are the one to lead the way with your entrepreneur skill to make the entire business successful.

The land is the premises where you will conduct your business

Capital are the necessary equipments including cash required to start and run the business. All these have to be put in place to make it work.

However if you are using the *Nothing Down Technique* in business, all these; land and capital can be gotten for *free* using the power of Negotiation.

- Third Question: Who And Who Does The Business Depend On For Survival.

These are the people responsible for start-ups, planning and execution of such business. Without such people, there will be no business in the first place. Some people believe their business doesn't depend on people, sorry to say, no business can survive without people. These people include: yourself, your partners, your investors, your employee and most importantly your customers which are the reason why you are in the business in the first place. Learn "*people skill*" and treat people well and you will see your business blossom. People skill is same as *Personal Success Skills* listed in chapter two.

- Most Important Of All Before Any Venture: Self Realization

Self realization is one of the greatest achievement and discovery one can have early in his or her life time. Everything that comes in and out from your life is determined by your *Self-concept*. To be brief about it, Self realization helps you to know your strengths, weaknesses, uniqueness and how to manage them or improve on them to make you a more effective and efficient person. You don't need to be ashamed of your weaknesses, because everybody has one. That's why there is a saying that states, '*No one is perfect*'. Yes no one is perfect, but some people are more efficient in their dealings

than others, this is why they are more
successful than the less efficient ones. Once
you identify your Strength and Uniqueness,
use them as often as you can and make them
your *'Selling Point' or 'Unique Selling Point'*.
Also when you identify your weaknesses,
acknowledge them and get someone to work
with you whose strength complement your
weaknesses and manage it properly.

You really need to work on this; it's the centre
of everything in your life.

★ ★ ★ ★ ★ ★ ★ ★ ★ ★
Entrepreneurs' note
Once you identify your Strength and Uniqueness, use
them as often as you can and make them your Unique
Selling Point
★ ★ ★ ★ ★ ★ ★ ★ ★ ★

3.1   An Entrepreneur's Mindset

An entrepreneur is someone who starts and operates a business venture, and assumes the responsibility for it. An entrepreneur provides goods and services to individuals and/or businesses for payment.

As an entrepreneur you have to believe in yourself. Believe in yourself, your abilities, your skills and your business. Be courageous and persistent. Be attentive and open-minded, good listening skills is a great asset. Creativity and innovation is always common with great entrepreneurs.

Be a goal getter. If you want to be efficient as other successful entrepreneur, you have to set achievable goals and work to achieve them.

Don't be afraid to set goals, even if you didn't meet your target fully, at least you should do your best to try and achieve it, knowing that you will do better the next time you try.

You have to inculcate the mindset of an Entrepreneur, you have to think the way they do, act the way they act, even dress the way that suit your business as other successful entrepreneurs in your fields do. Appearance matters a lot, so is first impression.

- Feasibility Study

  Before venturing into any form of business, one has to do what is called feasibility study and market survey. This projects how lucrative a business can be now and in the near future.

It measures parameters such as:

- ➤ Demand and Supply,

- ➤ The Market and Pricing,

- ➤ Availability and Scarcity of Products and Services etc.

Without feasibility study and market survey, one is trading/venturing without foresight and vision. Such business will be moving in circles. Always do a feasibility study before venturing into any business.

Don't be afraid of the term *feasibility study.* It can be as easy as taking a sheet of paper, strolling around the vicinity you want to set-up your business and writing your personal observations and that of residents in the area. It could just take an hour or two for this study or months of feasibility study and planning depending on the business you are venturing

into.

4   10 SIMPLE AND PRACTICABLE STEPS TO STARTING A BUSINESS

Starting a business involves planning, making key financial decisions and completing a series of legal activities. These 10 easy steps can help you plan, prepare and manage your business. Here we are going to discuss it briefly.

Step 1: Write a Business Plan

Don't let the word 'Business Plan' scare you. Writing a business plan is the same as stating (writing) what you intend to achieve in that business and how you will achieve it. It works with the following:

- ➢ Your present situation?
- ➢ Your Future projection?

> ➢ The required process to get there (Future)?

Don't let those ROI, and other ratios confuse you yet.
With a proper answering of these, you are good to go
for starters and less complex business, but for more
complex biz, a lot of parameters need to be
considered and taken care of.

Step 2: Get Business Training and Assistance

Take courses, read books, audio tapes and Training
on business and get expert advice as you are doing
now.

Step 3: Choose a Business Location

Location is very important to the success of a business, if you are in a good location you will get good traffic without much work on advert, the reverse is the case for a bad location.

Step 4: Finance Your Business

Get loan and grants to finance your business. Use the following channels

- Personal financing

- Bank loans

- Government grants

- Family/friends loans/contributions etc

Step 5: Determine the Legal Structure of Your Business

You have to decide which form of ownership is best for you: sole proprietorship, partnership, Limited Liability Company (LLC), corporation, non-profit or cooperative.

Step 6: Register a Business Name

Register your business name with your state government in your locality.

Step 7: Get a Tax Identification Number

To pay Tax, Learn which tax identification number you'll need to obtain from the IRS and your state revenue agency.

Step 8: Register for State and Local Taxes

Register with your state to obtain a tax identification number, workers' compensation, unemployment and disability insurance.

Step 9: Obtain Business Licenses and Permits

Get a list of federal, state and local licenses and permits required for your business.

Step 10: Understand Employer Responsibilities

Know what you have to do as an employer and delegate the appropriate responsibilities to your employees while sticking to the core responsibility of your business.

Action Exercise

1. Write what being in business means to you (your personal motivation for being in business)?

2. Write the benefit you and your products and services can offer your customers to bring about "mutual benefit" to both parties.

3. List your strengths, weaknesses and Uniqueness and state how you can use your

strength and uniqueness to successfully

operate your business.

Decide to operate from your *Strength Zone*.

4. Imbibe the Entrepreneur's Mindset; get close

to other successful entrepreneur and learn

additional skills that make them successful in

their business.

5. Do a feasibility study on your

present/proposed business; measuring the

following:

> - Demand and Supply

> - The Market Trend and pricing

> - Availability and scarcity of products

> and services etc.

SECTION B:

GROWING A

BUSINESS

FOR

PROFIT

5 GROWING A BUSINESS FOR PROFIT

If you have already started your business, I must say a big congratulation to you, you have done the

> Obstacles are those frightful things you see when you take your eyes off your goals – Henry Ford

hard part. The part most people are afraid of is starting, as Don Shula quoted

"The start is what stops most people – Don Shula".

You have done what most people are afraid to do and you should be proud of it.

However it doesn't stop there, the next challenge is how to make your business grow and profit from it.

Below are some easy steps you can use to get the

desired profit and put your business on track.

5.1   Employee Motivation

Employee has to be constantly motivated and

happy with their job. If they are not happy

with their job or work, the work will feel

boring to them and this will reflect on their

productivity. This will also be seen by

customers who will one way or another try to

avoid such employee or avoid your

company/business outlet entirely. People

want to shop and do business in a place that

makes them feel happy and cares about them.

Also watch out for employee with BAD

ATTITUDES and or NEGATIVITY. These

people are capable of crippling your business

in a very short time and will suffocate it from

blossoming or seeing the light of day.

Treat employee nice, motivate them and pay

them well to the best of your company ability

and their productivity. Lazy people should be

avoided.

5.2   Advertise Your Business

Get people to know and talk about your

business. The more people know about it the

more potential customers you will have. The

more potential customers you have; the

higher the chances of getting more sales.

Wherever you are and whatever you do, let

people know about what you do, what your

business is all about and how your business

can help them or their friends.

You can do personal advertising or paid

advertising, it doesn't matter as long as it's

advertising.

Please note: *a business that is not known is*

nonexistent to potential customers who haven't

heard about such business.

5.3   Clear Cut Point Of Sale

Point of sale is where the products are

exchanges for money or financial

remuneration in cash, barter or kind. This has

to be well defined, so that all the hard work of

getting customers in and execution will not be wasted.

Even if you are giving out free items to people, the aim should be to attract them to buy other products from you and make them your customer. Anything short of this will make you broke in no time.

Remember it is a business you are running, the more you sell the more profit you make, the more your business grows and this is why the point of sale is very important.

5.4   Innovation And Creativity

Innovation and creativity should be a driving force in any business outlet, keep pushing for more. Constantly better your bests. When you reach one milestone, reward yourself and push for more because if you don't, life will move ahead of you, overtake you and leave you behind. A great wisdom quotes gives a good scenario of it and it quotes:

'It takes all the running you can do to keep in the same place. If you want to get somewhere else, you must run at least twice as fast as that! – (the Queen of Hearts in Alice in Wonderland)'

5.5   Important Realities About Business

And Life

Remember, the only thing constant is life is

CHANGE. So when things change in a

different and difficult way, change to catch-

up and be updated. The ultimate rule is

ADAPTATION AND SURVIVAL.

Note: *we cannot change the direction and*

intensity of the Wind, but we can direct the Sail of

our boat using the wind.

Chaos is only meant to stop those that are not

strong enough to handle it. Understand that

every problem as a challenge and an

opportunity for greater success/achievements

when solved.

Be productive, be successful, be the best you

can be...

Action Exercise

1. Decide today to motivate your employees to

   give out their best.

2. Let your *'point of sale'* be clearly visible and

   efficient.

3. Decide to be creative and innovative in your

   business; find better and more effective ways

   to conduct business.

4. Decide today to tell almost everyone you

    come across about your business and what

    your products can offer them.

SECTION C:

BONUS SECTIONS

(OTHER

PARAMETER TO

MAKE YOU AND

YOUR BUSINESS

SUCCESSFUL)

FIVE TIPS ON HOW TO DEVELOP GREAT START-UPS NAME

A Great company name isn't just about finding something that sounds right.

In starting a business, what you may call a new venture can very well turn out to be one of the most important decisions you will make in the early days of a company. The business name will dictate which Web domain you can register, your trademark, and how people identify what you do, your business identity impression and other things associated with the business.

Here are five things to keep in mind.

1. Watch out for sound-alikes.

When starting a business you have to avoid a name that has too many alternate spellings. For example, you might want to call your new start-up Phaser, but note that too many people will think it is Fazer or Faser. They will type that domain into a browser and find the wrong brand. This will reduce the amount of business you will get.

2. Wait for the 'Aha' moment.

Do a brainstorming session with friends and family, write down as many interesting words as possible. When you get the work that match the business identity you want, pronounce it as much as you can, when you feel the "Aha" moment, it means you are on track." As a Start-up, you should take some time saying the words out loud because you are going to be saying it a lot: on the phone, in face-to-face meetings, in presentations. You want your words to easily translate to the keyboard for accuracy and ease'. If it feels right to you and others who help you come up with the name, chances are it will feel right to your potential customers.

3. Let your name tell a story.

When your company name tells a story about itself

or it origin or your business activities it can help with

branding and it is sure to generate a lot of buzz.

4. Make it personal.

When picking a name, you can pick something that appeal to your personality or personal life. Your company name is often an extension of your personality. Caroline Fielding was doodling on a sheet of paper one night, trying to think of a company name. She thought about three grandsons in the family: Dean, Bryan, and Steven. And, she thought about how her company, which makes an iPhone app called Bus Rage, is driven to succeed. She combined the three names to create Dryven. "The name is easier to remember [for customers] when there is a personal story behind it," she says, and so can yours.

5. Make sure you love it.

The process of picking a name can easily turn into a huge headache for most people. A businessman tells a story of him and his partner; says he and a business partner spent hundreds of hours thinking of a name. They went through a laundry list of Greek gods, mountain ranges, and geographic locations but came up empty. He decided to pick a known quantity: the street he lives on, Kingdom Ridge. He now says the name resonates with him every time he hears it.

7 4 Ways to Boost Your Company's Value

Continuous effort, not strength or intelligence, is the key to unlock your potential - Winston Churchill

Boosting your company's value is an art of growing and preparing your company to a point where investors' can invest in it or you can maybe sell it for huge profit if you wish or still keep it as yours. Seneca, a first-century Roman philosopher once observed, *"Luck is where the crossroads of opportunity and preparation meet."* Some business owners believe they'll be able to "get lucky" and sell their companies for higher than the market average. While luck never hurts, preparation is critical if you want to secure a higher price for your company.

"Luck is where the crossroads of opportunity and

preparation meet – Seneca."

Successful middle market business owners have

dedicated their lives to building their companies.

They understand their industry, are keenly aware of

the competition, know how to serve customers and

have developed well trained, capable management

teams. Most of what they have accomplished is a

result of hard work, not luck.

Surprisingly, 65 percent of these same owners do not

know how much their business is worth and 85

percent do not have an exit plan. In essence they are

relying on fate with a healthy dose of luck to

ultimately secure a premium price for their company

should they exit by choice.

Experience has taught us that managing these four variables helps to replace luck with strategic preparedness in securing a premium price for your business:

1. Your organization should not be dependent on any one person: If the future success of your business is dependent upon a few star employees or one person on the leadership team, it can impact the financial potential of the company and could degrade valuation. Ensure your company has great processes in place that could be executed by others if necessary. This makes it easier for a potential buyer or investor to envision how the company could continue to grow and expand even without the current owners or key employees.

2. Your establishment should be recognized as a great place to work.

Investors are attracted to companies that are great places to work. The employees are excited and happy, and turnover is low. Their compensation packages are fair and tied to performance. The company should strive for a reputation of honesty, fairness, and ability to deliver. In great companies, the employees feel lucky to work there and the owners will benefit when it is time to find investors or sell the business comes.

3. Your company should have at least three growth markets identified at all times.

Companies, that sell for higher prices or secure the capital they need to expand, can demonstrate they will continue to grow. Investors are looking for an opportunity to make money. One proven way to make money is to invest in companies that are growing and will continue to grow in the future. To ensure future growth, owners need to adapt to changing technology, identify new markets, and continually train the workforce. Attractive companies know where they are going and have a definite plan to get there.

Companies who are attractive to potential investors or buyers seek out good advisors across all fronts. They seek the advice of experienced financial advisors, lawyers, HR consultants, and investment bankers. They're among the 15% who have an exit plan in place and probably have had the plan in place for a long time. Their financial records are in order. They do not have any pending legal issues. They have a solid understanding of what their company is worth and they have clear personal and financial goals.

4. Your company should have at least one proprietary product or procedure.

Smart business owners develop new methods to accomplish everyday jobs in a more efficient manner. Really smart owners patent those methods or technology so they own it and it cannot be duplicated by a competitor. This concept is proven almost daily when technology companies that have not even made money, sell for millions and sometimes billions. Owning proprietary technology or patents is a great way to boost the value of your company and attract investors.

If an owner has built a strong, successful company
with a great future, the likelihood that they will "get
lucky" and sell for a much higher price is much more
likely. They've simply followed the advice of the
Roman philosopher, Seneca. They were prepared
when the right opportunity became available.

Action exercise

1. If you are about to start/name a business, you
   can use the strategy listed in chapter six (6).
   You can also hold a brainstorming session to
   come-up with great names.
2. Apply the strategy in chapter seven (7) to
   attract financing, investors and increase
   growth.

Congratulations

You have come to the end of this training manual on how to start and grow a business for profit. All that is required from you now is to take action. Don't wait for the perfect moment, create the perfect moment. Don't wait for the tide, set sail and you will catch up with the tide.
There is no better day to start your business and make more profit than today. Take appropriate action right now and watch your business come alive and excel in every way.

Journey to Success

It is important to note that every big, sophisticated,

money generating business started from a less rosy

point different from the boom and profit making

point where they are currently. Some started broke,

with little or no resources. But it took hard work and

dedication from the founders (entrepreneurs) and

workers to make it what it is today.

So my advice is: if you don't have huge capital, Start small and Grow your Business to where it needs to be.

The big corporations you admire today, the multi-billion dollar investments; Microsoft, Trump Organization, Virgin Group, Dangote Group etc. were not at this admirable state when they started. Some of them started from their own backyard, garage, some others the kitchen, living rooms, dining or reading table etc. Yours can start from where you are right now; it's a matter of desire, will power and persistency.

Start Today and you will be amazed at what you will discover and achieve only if you just take that bold step.

I will leave you with this quote from the first ever billionaire in dollars John D. Rockefeller:

I do not think there is any other quality so essential to success of any kind as the quality of perseverance. It overcomes almost everything, even Nature - John D. Rockefeller

Don't forget to be productive with your time and resources; if you are productive, you are sure to be successful in your endeavours. Continuous improvement in your abilities will propel you to go higher and higher to be the best you desire to be.

Therefore;

Be productive   Be successful   Be the best you

can be...